FREDERICK DOUGLASS

Portrait of a Freedom Fighter

by Sheila Keenan

SCHOLASTIC INC.

New York Toronto London Auckland Sydney

Thanks to Cathy Ingram at the Frederick Douglass National Historic Site in Washington, D.C., for her kind assistance.

— S.K.

Photo Credits

Front cover: The Bettman Archives. Back cover: Culver Pictures.

The American Antiquarian Society: p. 20 (Frederick Douglass' Paper); The Bettman Archives: pp. 5, 22 (Fourth Colored Infantry); Culver Pictures: pp. 6, 11, 25, 31; The Granger Collection: pp. 3, 12, 15 (Susan B. Anthony), 20 (North Star masthead), 32; Library of Congress: p. 9; © Media Plus, Inc.: p. 19; Moorland-Spingarn Research Center, Howard University: p. 28; National Park Service, Frederick Douglass National Historic Site: p. 23 (Lewis Douglass); National Portrait Gallery, Smithsonian Institution/ Art Resource, NY: p. 1; New-York Historical Society, New York City: p. 27; New York Public Library: pp. 4, 15 (Wm. Lloyd Garrison, Wendell Phillips), 16, 23 (Charles Douglass), 24; North Wind Picture Archives: p. 23 (Colored Troops Banner); Sophia Smith Collection, Smith College: p. 15 (Sojourner Truth).

ISBN 0-590-48356-0

Copyright © 1995 by Scholastic Inc.
All rights reserved. Published by Scholastic Inc.

12 11 10 9 8 7 6 5 4   7 8 0/0 9

Printed in the U.S.A.   24

First Scholastic printing, January 1995

Imagine not knowing when your birthday is. Imagine not knowing who your parents are. Imagine someone owning you, just as one owns a dog or a horse or a mule.

Frederick Douglass didn't have to imagine these things. That's what it was like to be a slave.

Frederick Augustus Washington Bailey was born sometime in February 1818, in Tuckahoe, Maryland. He later changed his last name to Douglass.

Slaves were normally given clothes only once
a year. Frederick's two coarse shirts, two pair
of pants, one jacket, one pair of socks, and one
pair of shoes had to last through an entire
year of hard work outdoors.

Most slaves lived in very small, rough cabins with dirt floors. With so few clothes, it was hard for the slaves to keep warm at night. Frederick used to sleep inside a grain bag. His feet dangled out in the cold.

Many slaves worked in cotton fields.

Once a day a big bowl of cornmeal mush was put out in the yard. Frederick and the other children grabbed at the food with their bare hands. Everyone always came away hungry.

Slaves worked from sunrise to sunset. Even young children like Frederick were kept busy working. If they didn't work hard enough, they would be whipped.

Cold, hunger, and fear were a big part of slave life. But what Frederick hated most was not being *free*.

When he was seven years old, Frederick was sent to Baltimore to work as a slave for the Auld family.

Mrs. Auld started to teach Frederick the ABC's. Mr. Auld quickly stopped her. She didn't know it was against the law to teach a slave to read. It was thought that if slaves could read, they would get too many ideas, and would become spoiled.

But Frederick wasn't going to stop learning!

Mrs. Auld teaching Frederick to read.

Frederick hid an old spelling book and taught himself to read it. He dared street boys to prove they knew the alphabet. The boys drew chalk letters on walls. Frederick copied all their letters.

Later, Frederick taught other black people to read and write in Sunday school.

Baltimore, Maryland, where Frederick lived with the Aulds.

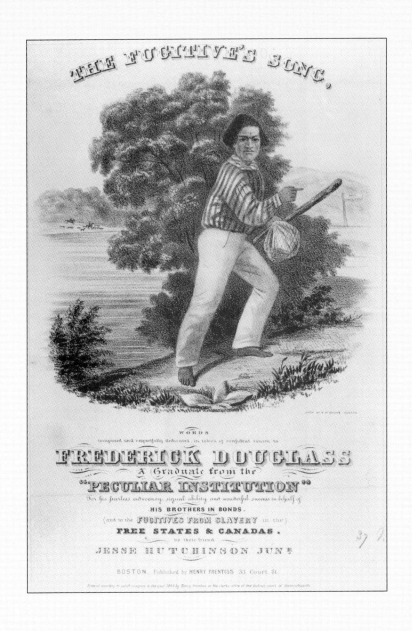

When he got older, Frederick worked as a shipbuilder. All the money he earned went to Mr. Auld.

"Why are some people masters?" Frederick often asked himself. "Why am I a slave?" Frederick couldn't stand it any longer. He decided to run away.

Frederick disguised himself as a sailor. He boarded a train for the first time in his life. The train took him north to New York City — and to *freedom*.

Frederick changed his last name to Douglass to be safe from slave hunters. A song was written about his daring escape.

While he was in New York, Frederick married a free woman he had met and fallen in love with in Baltimore. He and Anna moved to Massachusetts and had the first of five children.

In 1841, Frederick Douglass went to an abolitionist convention. Abolitionists were people who fought to end slavery. To his surprise, he was asked to speak. Frederick stood up and talked about his life as a slave. By the end of his speech, he was the new hero of the abolitionists.

Some famous abolitionists

William Lloyd Garrison   editor

Sojourner Truth   ex-slave

Susan B. Anthony   feminist

Wendell Phillips   lawyer

Being an abolitionist was often dangerous.

Frederick Douglass traveled to one hundred public meetings around the country. He spoke about the cruelty of slave life.

Some people who came to the meetings did not believe slaves should be free. Name-calling, egg-throwing, and fistfights sometimes broke out. But Frederick Douglass kept on traveling and kept on talking about how wrong slavery was.

Frederick Douglass was a powerful speaker.
His words and stories often made people cry.
Other people said no one who had really
been a slave could make such great speeches.
Frederick wanted to prove they were wrong.

Frederick decided to write down the story
of his life. His book would tell where he was
born. It would tell the name of the master
who still owned him. Douglass' friends sent
$700 to Mr. Auld to "buy" the freedom of
the most famous black man in the United States.

Second Book

As related in the preceding chapter, my free life began on the third of september 1838. On the morning of the 4th of that month, after an anxious, perilous, but safe journey I came in the city of Newyork a free man, one more added to the mighty throng which like the confused waves of a troubled sea, surged too and fro between the lofty walls of Broadway. Though dazzled with the wonders of the great city, my thoughts could not be much withdrawn from my strange situation. For the moment the dreams of my youth, the hopes of my manhood were completely fulfilled. The bonds that held me to old master were broken. No man now had a right to call me his slave or assert mastery over me. I have often been asked how I felt when first I found myself upon free soil, and my readers may share the same curiosity. There is scarcely anything in

Douglass' notes for a book about his life.

THE NORTH STAR.

RIGHT IS OF NO SEX—TRUTH IS OF NO COLOR—GOD IS THE FATHER OF US ALL, AND ALL WE ARE BRETHREN.

VOL. I. NO. 1. ROCHESTER, N. Y., FRIDAY, DECEMBER 3, 1847. WHOL

Frederick Douglass' Paper.

DEVOTED TO THE RIGHTS OF ALL MANKIND, WITHOUT DISTINCTION OF COLOR, CLASS, OR CLIME.

VOL. X.---NO. 48. ROCHESTER, N. Y., NOVEMBER 13, 1857. WHOLE NO. 516.

FREDERICK DOUGLASS' PAPER.
IS PUBLISHED EVERY FRIDAY MORNING,
At No. 25, Buffalo Street, (opposite the Arcade,) Rochester N. Y.

TERMS OF SUBSCRIPTION.

Single copies, one year (invariably in advance,) $1 50; five copies and over $5 00.

POSTAGE.—Inside of Monroe County, free ; to any part of New York State payable in advance, 3 cts. to any part of the United States, 6 cts. per quarter.

Selected.

THE EXILED NEGROES OF CANADA.

Report of The Tribune's Special Commissioner.

I.

THE NEGROES OF TORONTO.

The neighboring British provinces have long been the refuge of the fugitive slave, and every increase on this side of the border of the rigor of the laws to ensure his return to his master causes him to look with more eager longing to a country in which his liberty is secure and he possesses the same political rights as the rest of mankind. There the law is a protector, and the public, always more rigidly virtuous when the crime to be condemned is that of a neighbor, will see that it is neither violated nor evaded. The desire of safety and of political equality, valued the more highly from its being strenuously denied, has attracted numbers of colored men, both fugitive slaves and free, to a climate naturally uncongenial to them. What has been the effects of this security and this political equality upon them? Have they improved morally and socially?—Have they become more industrious and more intelligent, or, in the absence of all restraint, have they become idler and more vicious?—Are they capable, under favorable circumstances, of becoming good citizens in a well ordered community, or is there a want in their organization which renders the overseer and the taskmaster necessary to their well-being? A hurried trip through a portion of Upper Canada, undertaken as a relaxation from professional toil and care, has enabled the writer to answer some of these questions, at least to his own satisfaction. He claims no peculiar fitness for his task beyond an honest desire to learn the truth, to see facts as they exist, uncolored as far as possible by prejudice or theory ; and if, with every well-wisher of his

open piano stood on one side of the room, a melodeon occupied the pier between the windows ; on the walls hung a well-painted portrait of the owner of the house, and engravings representing the Queen, her husband and children. Though early in September, the evening being somewhat cool, a small woodfire blazed upon the hearth. Our host was a light-colored mulatto of middle age, short, spare, well and strongly built, with a large square head and a firm, sagacious looking countenace.—Many years previous he had emigrated, with his wife and elder children, from Mobile, bringing some capital with him. He was by trade a carpenter, and industry, economy and judicious investments had gradually raised him to his present position. His wife, apparently in ill health, was darker than himself; the children, somewhat darker, too, than the father, consisted of a well-built lad of 19, a slender girl of 17 and a boy of 12, who was busy at the table writing a school exercise. The elder boy was studying medicine, and, at the same time preparing himself to pass the classical examination, which, in Upper Canada, is a necessary preliminary to taking the degree of Doctor of Medicine, and had advanced so far as to read Cicero De Senectute. The language of the young people was correct and well chosen, and both in manner and conversation they would be looked upon as good examples of the youth of the middle class of any nation. In the course of the evening the young man played several pieces on the piano, and he and his sister sang duets with skill and taste.

The physician, Dr. A. T. A., is a mulatto, a native of Virginia, but for a long time resident in Philadelphia. Finding that he was unable to obtain access to the medical schools in that city, he came to Toronto and entered there upon the study of medicine, attending the lectures of the faculty of medicine of Trinity College. He has not yet obtained a degree, since though he passed a creditable examination in medicine, he failed in the classical examination, which is a necessary preliminary to graduation. He is now prepared for this ordeal, and, after being examined again upon the prescribed books of Plato and Cicero, and translating the necessary amount of good English into bad Latin, will become an M. D. He, however, is already engaged in practice, and has received the appointment of Physician to the Poor-house, which, as it is in the gift of medical men, is a proof of the advancement he has made. He both talks and writes well, and is generally respected throughout the city.

The livery-stable keeper is a fine example,

Of these, 78 only were coloured—not 1½ per cent. Now, as the coloured people constitute, at the lowest computation, between two and three per cent. of the total population of Toronto, this is a high and, I may add, an unexpected evidence of the general good conduct of the coloured people ; and the value of it is increased when we remember that they all originally belonged to the class in which crime against order and property are the most rife. Of the whole number of persons arrested, 4,295 were males and 1,051, or nearly one-fourth, were females ; while of the colored people 70 were males and 8 only, not quite one-ninth, were females.

The printed report of Mr. Sherwood refers, as was stated, to the total number of arrests. Of these, 1,922 were summarily punished by fine, in 273 cases the charges were withdrawn, and 230 cases were dismissed. Thinking that possibly the actual commitments to jail might set a different face upon the matter, we obtained from Mr. George L. Allan, the intelligent keeper of the jail at Toronto, the monthly return of commitments to that prison from October 1, 1855, to July 31, 1857, a period of twenty-two months, transcribing them from the books of the jail in his presence. The total commitments amounted in that period to 3,370, of whom 62, not quite two per cent., were coloured. Immediately after the passage of our Fugitive Slave law, Mr. Allan informed us that there was a sudden increase in the number of commitments among the coloured people, almost wholly for petty larcenies. This increase of crime Mr. A. attributed to the number of fugitives who flocked into Canada without any means of support and whom destitution drove to theft ; in a few months, as the new-comers found employment, this increase disappeared. On the whole, Mr. Allan was decided, in the opinion that, as regards crime against the law, the condi ion of the coloured people was better than that of the mass of the population.

II.

THE NEGROES OF HAMILTON AND CHATHAM.

At Hamilton, in a population of 24,000, there are from 400 to 600 colored people, among them blacksmiths, carpenters, plasterers and one wheelwright. There are two churches, small frame buildings, a Baptist and a Methodist, but they are not well supported, and neither of them at present has a regular resident clergyman. Many of the colored men are reputed to possess property, but I do not

little outward appearance of wealth. For the first time in my travels the women were without hoops, and some strapping lassies I met, covered with huge flat Bloomer hats, their naturally broad shoulders rendered broader by a cape, their clinging skirts, innocent of starch, brass or whalebone, presented to one fresh from the city a sight sufficiently strange. Here at last was an inversion of the common order of things! The principal hotel at which we put up was a large, wooden barrack of a building, the entrance on a level with the unpaved street, and sharing necessarily somewhat its color and appearance. Inside, things were more inviting ; the rooms were clean, neat and comfortable, and the beds, except that they were stuffed with feathers, irreproachable. We found the landlord, a huge, jolly Englishman, at the head of his own tea-table, carving a round of beef big enough to have fed the Common Council of a city ; and, for the first time since we had been in Canada, in a place swarming with negroes, the waiters at table were white, and females. The town consists of one long street—King street—closely built, in which the stores are all situated, while the dwellings, mostly surrounded by gardens, are scattered over streets crossing and running parallel to it.

Despite its unpromising appearance, Chatham seems an active and stirring place. In the town there are three saw-mills, two shingle-mills, two potash factories, two sash and blind factories, four flour-mills, four brick-yards, several iron-founderies, three or four wagon factories, three cabinet warehouses, three breweries and two distilleries. It is a port of entry, and exports a large amount of lumber, staves, shingles, bricks, drain tiles and flour. A large steamboat was, when we were there, being loaded for Buffalo, and two smaller steamers and a brig were lying in the stream. Before the present depression in business, which prevails equally in Canada as in the United States, seven steamboats and a dozen sailing vessels have been seen in the port at one time, completely filling up the river.

Of this busy town about one-third of the population are colored people, and they appear to contribute their full quota towards its industry. Among them are one gunsmith, four cabinet-makers working on their own account and employing others, six master carpenters, a number of plasterers, three printers, two watchmakers, two ship-carpenters, two millers, four blacksmiths, one upholsterer, one saddler, six master shoemakers, six grocers, and a cigar-maker. Unskilled workmen find abundant employment in the various mills, in agricultural labor and in cutting

tion and culture than among the same class at Toronto.

In Kent, the County in which Chatham is situated, many of the coloured people are agriculturists, residing upon and cultivating their own farms. Many of them are represented as doing exceedingly well. One farm, owned and occupied by a coloured man recently deceased, and still cultivated by his family, was generally allowed by those not disposed to favor the blacks, as well as by their well-wishers, to be the model farm of the neigh[illegible]d. Some, without capital or skill, and [illegible]ably, too, without sustained industry, do not succeed ; but it is generally admitted that, on the whole they make better farmers than the Irish, and far better than the French Canadians, a considerable number of whom reside in the immediate neighborhood of Chatham.

From the Liberator.

Memorial of the Colored Citizens of Wisconsin :

To the Honorable, the Legislature of the State of Wisconsin.

We, the undersigned, colored inhabitants of the State of Wisconsin, would once more exercise the *right*, which is guaranteed to *all the people*, peaceably to assemble, and petition the Government for a redress of Grievances. We complain of Art. 3d, Sec. 1st of the Constitution of the State of Wisconsin. We now ask your honorable body to regard our feeble request, and remove this *heel of oppression* and disability which rests upon us, as contained in the Article and section referred to, and thereby gives us an opportunity to become respected citizens of the State. We complain of that part of the Section which disallows to us the right of franchise and at the same time grants it to others who immigrate from foreign lands, and who do not understand the Constitution, Government and Laws as well as ourselves. We do not say, neither do we *believe*, that men of foreign birth, immigrating to this asylum of the oppressed, should be deprived of any of the rights and blessings which this government has confirmed upon them ; but we *do* say, that the same rights and blessings should be extended to us. In addition to all this, is it not proper to submit to your honorable body to say if it be right justice, or *common sense*, that we should be subject to taxation without representation?

We are informed—by those who claim to know—that a vote was taken by the people in 1849, and that a majority of votes were cast in favor of suffrage—thereby taking away

siderable section of it. At all events, Kansas is at this moment suffering in many other particulars under the incubus of Border-Ruffian legislation, from which her people are entitled to be relieved at the earliest possible moment.—[*New York Tribune.*

SLAVERY IN THE STATE OF NEW YORK.

Through the Lemmon case, just argued in our First Judicial District, the "National Democracy" has delivered its Laws and its Politics respecting Slavery in the State of New York. In the lengthy argument of Charles O'Conor, pleading for Virginia and for the right of property in man, the following points were deliberately taken, and boldly maintained. The free men of New York can see the condition to which "Democracy" is determined to bring the Empire State :

"The ancient general or common law of this State authorized the holding of negroes as slaves therein. The Judiciary never had any constitutional power to annul, repeal, or set aside, this law.

"The Judiciary never had any power to annul, repeal, or set aside, the slave law of this State, which we have shown existed with the sanction of the Legislature prior to the Revolution.

"The Judicial department has no right to declare Negro Slavery to be contrary to the law of nature, or immortal, or unjust, or to take any measure, or to introduce any policy, for the suppression of it, founded on any such ideas.

"It cannot be pretended that there ever was in England, or that there now is in any State of the Union, a law, by any name, thus outlawing slavery. The common law of all these countries has always regarded it as a basis of individual rights.

"In fact there is no violation of the principles of enlightened justice, nor any departure from the dictates of pure benevolence, in holding negroes in a state of slavery.

"Negroes, alone and aided by the guardianship of another race, cannot sustain a civilized social state.

"Who shall deny the claim of the intellectual white race to its compensation for the mental toil of governing and guiding the negro laborer?

"It follows, that in order to obtain the measure of reasonable personal enjoyment, and of usefulness to himself and others, for which he is adapted by nature, the negro

The Douglass family moved to Rochester, New York. Frederick started his own newspaper. He named it after the star that runaway slaves followed north to freedom, the North Star. Douglass published *The North Star* for seventeen years.

The North Star printed stories written by black people about abolition, and equal rights for women.

Black soldiers at Fort Lincoln.

In 1861, the Civil War began. The North and South went to war over slavery and states' rights. Black men were not allowed to join the North's army. Douglass spoke out against this. Three years later, his own sons were among the first black men to serve in the Civil War.

Lewis Henry Douglass was
a sergeant major in the
Union Army.

Charles Redmond Douglass
was a private.

Frederick Douglass was the first black person
to go to a White House reception.

Black soldiers were paid less than white soldiers. They
got the more dangerous jobs, too.

Douglass visited President Lincoln to discuss these
problems. The two tall, distinguished men, one an ex-slave,
one the president of the United States, met at the White
House. President Lincoln promised to see about an
increase in pay for black soldiers.

After the Civil War, slavery was made illegal in the United States.

Frederick Douglass was now forty-eight years old. He had fought against slavery for over twenty years. Now slaves were free by law, but were not *equal* under the law. Douglass began a new fight.

Laws in the South kept black people living just like slaves. Many were beaten or killed for trying to vote.

The former slave, who had taught himself to read, now had his own library with over two thousand books.

For the next thirty years, Frederick Douglass gave speeches and wrote articles about equal rights. He advised presidents and politicians. Douglass was appointed marshal of the District of Columbia. He was the first black person to hold this job. Later he became the minister to Haiti.

On February 20, 1895, in the same month he had been born a slave seventy-seven years earlier, Frederick Douglass died in his own home — a free man, a famous man, a hero.

Frederick Douglass' former home in Washington, D.C., is now a museum.

FREDERICK DOUGLASS
1818 – 1895
Freedom Fighter